Old London

Illustrated

Old London

ILLUSTRATED

Drawings by

H. W. BREWER

A Builder Book

THE BUILDER LTD

Builder House, 4 Catherine Street, London, W.C. 2.

Ninth Edition 1962

© *The Builder*

Printed in Great Britain by Tonbridge Printers Ltd, Peach Hall Works, Shipbourne Road, Tonbridge, Kent, and bound by
The Newdigate Press Ltd., Vincent Lane, Dorking, Surrey.

Foreword

It has been said that writing the history of a vast city like London is like writing a history of the ocean—the area is so vast, its inhabitants are so multifarious, the treasures that lie in its depth so countless.

Boswell once remarked " London is to the politician merely a seat of Government, to the Grazier a cattle market, to the merchant a huge exchange, to the dramatic enthusiast a congeries of theatres, to the man of pleasure an assemblage of Taverns." Boswell in his wisdom, was no doubt right, but to those who would wish to obtain a vision in words and pictures of what London was really like in olden days I commend this beautiful little volume.

I am writing this Foreword from the top of the 13th Century Bell Tower in the Tower of London. To the West there stretches out the whole panorama of the City of London flanked by London's great waterway the Thames. Southwards across the Pool of London lies Southwark with its great Cathedral, and Eastwards beyond Tower Bridge the river flows down to Greenwich. Behind me over the mellow tiles of Queen's House appear the four turrets of the White Tower built by William the Conqueror as a Citadel to defend the City.

As one gazes down on the London of today one tries to visualise what the old City looked like as Shakespeare knew it before the Great Fire consumed so great an area.

This fascinating book, built as it is, round the exquisite drawings of H. W. Brewer shows just what it was like. Little imagination is needed, as the pictures and descriptions are studied, to conjure up the scene of mediaeval London.

The dome of St. Paul's glitters in the sunlight beyond the Monument—close the eyes, the Monument disappears and the old St. Paul's emerges in all its majesty and grandeur, dominating the surrounding spires as it rises 500 feet towards the sky.

A clear picture is in the mind. The pages of the book are turned and the inside of the Cathedral in all its former glory passes before the eyes. And so it is with every drawing, Old London is reborn.

Perhaps of all the brilliant drawings which Brewer has given us the greatest is that of St. Stephen's Chapel at Westminster, which was for centuries the home of the Mother of Parliaments.

To study Old London Illustrated is indeed an enthralling experience.

COLONEL SIR THOMAS BUTLER, D.S.O., O.B.E., J.P.
Resident Governor of H.M. Tower of London

Contents

Plates

By H. W. Brewer (except as stated).

PREFACE

WITHIN fifty years of his death, Shakespeare's prophecy had come almost literally true of the City of London. It is the largely Mediaeval London he knew that is pictured

The cloud-capped towers, the gorgeous palaces,
The solemn temples, the great globe itself,
Yea, all which it inherit, shall dissolve,
And, like this insubstantial pageant faded,
Leave not a rack behind.

PROSPERO, *The Tempest.*

in the drawings of H. W. Brewer reproduced in this book, the London that virtually disappeared in the Great Fire of 1666—a London not only of " gorgeous palaces " and splendid monastic institutions, churches, civic buildings, gateways and private mansions as well as a great Norman Tower, a fine Cathedral and a fantastic old bridge, but of inns and shops and squalid if picturesque huddles of poor dwellings.

The fate of many of the buildings that survived the Fire was to be either demolished in the inevitable reconstruction of London, or destroyed or damaged in the war of 1939-45; but despite all the losses, many vestiges of Mediaeval London still remain, and Brewer shows how they looked in their contemporary settings.

Visitors to London, and especially those from overseas, desire some vision of the legendary and picturesque London that existed before the Dissolution of the Monasteries by Henry VIII and the Great Fire: they want to find traces of its ancient buildings, many of which survive only in name; and for these purposes they are admirably served by Brewer's drawings and writings.

Prior to the Dissolution, the City contained a great number of ecclesiastical buildings, many of which are still represented in the larger City of to-day. Of the larger monastic institutions some nineteen within and around the City are mentioned in the descriptions of the drawings, but there were also many smaller religious houses which were either destroyed or converted to other purposes; to say nothing of the great mediaeval buildings at Westminster, which Brewer also recorded.

For more than a quarter of a century until his death in 1903 at the age of sixty-seven, H. W. Brewer, one of the most gifted and prolific pictorial artists of his time, was a highly valued contributor to the artistic and literary departments of " The Builder." He began his artistic career in the days of wood engraving, his earliest work being merely illustrative of existing buildings; but with the introduction of photo-lithography and process engraving he realised that there was a wider field for an architectural artist in black-and-white than mere representation, and he took up two new lines of illustration, one the invention of architectural scenes purely with a view to picturesque effect, and the other, the restoration in drawings of cities and monuments of the past which had disappeared, but for the reconstruction of which a certain amount of documentary evidence could be found. To the first task he brought genius and imagination; to the second (as represented in this book) learning and research.

Brewer was a devout Catholic, to which fact may be traced, no doubt, his special interest in the remains of extinct mediaeval abbeys and other religious institutions. He spared no trouble in obtaining material for his restorations. Some of his sources of information were the engravings left to us by such sixteenth- and seventeenth-century artists as Wyngaerde, Agas, Haiward and Gascoyne, Norden, Visscher and Hollar.

The descriptive articles accompanying the drawings have been brought up to date as far as possible, but it has to be remembered that replanning, rebuilding or restoration are constantly going on. Brewer's remarkable work of re-creation stands, to provide a fascinating picture of Mediaeval London.

9

I. The City of London

THE City in the time of Henry VIII, (Plates 3 and 4), lies before us in panorama from the east. In the foreground stands the Tower, surrounded by the moat, which is shown as connected with the City ditch and the river. It should be mentioned, however, that the contours exclude the possibility that the moat and the City ditch could have been on the same level, and Plate II shows them correctly separated.

In those days the Tower still fulfilled its original Norman purpose of dominating the City. As will be seen from the illustration, the river was the great highway; and we note its broad water-course from Westminster, past Whitehall (the new Palace of Henry VIII), Scotland Place (the Palace of the Scottish Kings, whose site is now occupied by Scotland Yard), and the town residences of Bishops and Nobles. There the Thames was " bordered by its gardens green." The Strand in those days was, as its name implies, only a marginal strip of indifferent roadway beside the waterway; it did, however, serve as a connection between Westminster and the City. Along the riverside of the City, we see next Baynard's Castle and then the wharves and harbours, and lastly Old London Bridge. We trace the City wall from Tower Hill, by Hounds-ditch, past Moorfields, and even on the west to the right of the Cathedral. Some of the City gates will be seen in later drawings, and the one great approach from the south, London Bridge, will be separately described, but it should be noted that the Bridge is thus illustrated at two periods. In the time of Henry VIII the Traitors' Gate was on the seventh pier from the south. In 1577 it was pulled down, and the gate at the south end of the Bridge became the Traitors' Gate, as will be seen in the later drawing. In place of the original Traitors' Gate, there was erected Nonesuch House, and Bridge House was built at the same time. These are described with the other drawing, Old London Bridge (Plate 5), of which the date is about 1600.

Old St. Paul's Cathedral, which is separately illustrated (Plate 6), occupies a central position in the drawing, but its spire is not the only one pointing heavenwards. Within the City there were no fewer than 107 Parish Churches; and of these 86 fell a prey to the flames in the Great Fire of 1666, as did also the Cathedral, the Guildhall, 44 Livery Halls, and 13,200 houses. The two districts of Aldgate and Bishopsgate alone escaped, and, being in the eastern portion of the City, are in the foreground of the view. Several buildings which survived the Fire and exist to this day may be identified in the picture. The Church of the Augustine Friars, which is known as Austin Friars, had then a lofty steeple, with choir and transepts, but after the Dissolution these were pulled down; the nave, however, was spared and devoted to foreign Protestants, and has been the property of the Dutch Reformed Church since 1550. This Church was destroyed by enemy action in 1940-41. Other Churches which survived are: St. Ethelburga's, the smallest and most quaint Church in the City of to-day, and Great St. Helen's, which contains the Nuns' Chapel of the priory that adjoined it. Of the Churches near Aldgate, there are those of St. Katherine Cree and St. Andrew Undershaft, in Leadenhall Street. These, with St. Olave's, Hart Street, and All Hallows Barking, near the Tower, make six Parish Churches within the City walls which escaped the Great Fire and still survive. It must be recorded, however, that the two last named were very seriously damaged by enemy action. St. Olave's was Pepys's Church and All Hallows has a 14th-Century crypt containing signs of a Saxon

Church. The great market, called Leaden Hall, at the junction of Cornhill and Leaden-hall Street, was the first point at which the Fire was prevented from making further progress. The western front, however, of this most important civic building was damaged. The Guildhall was burnt out and left roofless, but the Crypt (1411), containing the priceless archives, was fortunately saved. In the raids of 1940 the Guildhall once more lost its roof. It has been rebuilt from the designs of the late Sir Giles Scott, R.A.

The Great Fire of 1666 originated near the City end of London Bridge, where it is commemorated by The Monument. It spread eastward to the foot of the Tower and right up to the north wall of the City. It was driven westward as far as the Temple Church, which was saved. That Church, built by the Knights Templars in circular form, and its 13th-Century addition, did not escape the fire following enemy action in 1940-41; however, its walls and beautiful Norman porch (1185) remain and some of its priceless marble effigies of Knights have been preserved. The Church has been restored under the direction of the late Walter H. Godfrey, F.S.A., F.R.I.B.A. Baynard's Castle, which dominated the City on the west (it may be recognised in the Plate by the flag on the tower at the waterside), had sufficient timber in its stone building to make it burn fiercely, and no part of it survived. London was left in 1666 a city of ruins; the Dissolution of the Monasteries had made it a city of names.

In the foreground of the picture, to the left of the Tower, will be seen the collegiate Church of St. Katherine, which disappeared in 1825 to make way for the dock which bears its name. It had a bell tower entirely separate from the Church. The big group of buildings to the right of the Tower ditch was called East Minster, in contrast with Westminster. The nave had beside it a choir of equal length, and a tower with steeple above it; the monastic buildings were to the north; there was a fine gateway facing west, and beyond it a Calvary Cross. Next to it was the very large Abbey, called St. Clare of The Minories. The last name remains to-day to denote the street on part of the site of the City ditch. It is said to be derived from the order of nuns called the Sorores Minores. The Abbey had a long choir, short nave and south transept, while on the north was a tower, crowned by a lantern, also cloisters and hall. These two Monastic institutions were both pulled down by Henry VIII, and to-day The Royal Mint occupies the site of the Minster. A similar fate befell the Monastery of the Crutched Friars, which might be reached by crossing the drawbridge spanning the City ditch and passing through the Postern Gate. The Crutched, or Crossed, Friar had a red cross on his back and carried an iron cross in his hand. To-day, part of Fenchurch Street Station crosses the street called Crutched Friars. The scaffold on Tower Hill, where so many political executions took place, will be noticed near the monastic buildings; the site is still marked on the green within the railings of Tower Hill Gardens.

The bridge over the City ditch, by St. Botolph's Church, Aldgate, led from White-chapel through the City gate into the precincts of the great Priory of the Holy Trinity. These are to be seen also in Plate 3. To the right of St. Botolph's, Aldgate, which had three naves of equal height and width and a fine tower with flying buttresses, the City ditch was called Houndsditch, and the street which now runs over the site bears that name. There was a mud wall on the eastern bank, and it is thought that this was built in order to prevent dogs and cats from being thrown into the ditch.

The next bridge over the ditch to be seen in Plate 4 connects Bishopsgate with the Church of St. Botolph, Bishopsgate, which stood "without." There were four City churches dedicated to this old English saint, each adjacent to a City gate. The one which has disappeared was at Billingsgate. Almost opposite St. Botolph's was St. Mary's Spital, which was a hospital and church in one; very much like St. Mary's Hospital at Chichester, which has tiny dwelling houses on each side of a central aisle and the Chapel at the end, all under one roof. Outside there was a preaching cross. The district is still known as Spitalfields. Next to St. Botolph's, Bishopsgate, was the Priory and Hospital of St. Mary of Bethlem. It was the grandmother, so to speak, of what is now the Royal Bethlem Hospital for the mentally afflicted, in South London, and popularly known as "Bedlam." Its original name is due to association with the Bishop of Bethlehem, who was entertained in the Priory by the monks whenever he came to London. The Hospital is now at Beckenham, Kent.

To the right of the next portion of the City ditch is what was then and still is known as Moorfields. Rising in its swampy ground and flowing through the City was a small stream, named Wall Brook. It still runs underground close by the line of the present Walbrook, the street which lies between the Mansion House and Cannon Street. Beyond Moorfields, outside the City wall, was an isolated fort said to be of Saxon origin called the Barbican, and the street which crosses its site to-day bears that name. Other buildings in the picture will appear in subsequent Plates.

II. The Tower of London

THE ancient defences of The Tower, which are well seen in Brewer's drawing, were four-fold. First from inside, there was the great Norman Keep; then an inner wall with twelve towers, all of which remain to-day; next, the outer wall, of which the bastions and towers are still tolerably perfect; and fourthly, on three sides, the Tower moat. The river formed the first line of defence on the south; the Wharf on that side was constructed by Henry III. The main approach was from the west (on the left of the illustration), where the Lion Gate stood. This name is due to the fact that lions and other wild animals were kept in the Lion Tower down to as late as 1834, when the collection formed the nucleus of the present Zoological Gardens. On each side of the drawbridge there was a Tower, viz., the Middle Tower first and then the Byward Tower, and these remain to-day. The Queen's Stairs, which are also seen on the left, were found to be a necessary addition. The river was the great highway, and when it brought important personages from Westminster the stairs gave access to the Palace by the bridge crossing the moat at the Byward Tower, thus avoiding the entrance by the ill-famed Traitors' Gate. There were also the Iron Gate at the east, near the wharf, giving access by the Develin Bridge (shown in Plate 3) crossing the moat, the water-gate in the Cradle Tower, and also the Traitors' Gate which still stands out towards the river in the centre of the wharf, and has over it St. Thomas's Tower. All these approaches led only to within the outer wall on the riverside, and entrance through the inner wall could be obtained only by the Garden Tower, or, as it has been called for the past 350 years, the Bloody Tower. The two modern entrances to the east of this were made for the convenience of the public and the military, respectively. The moat was drained in 1843, and part of it is used as a recreation and parade ground.

The Bell Tower, with its conspicuous wooden turret, in which hung the bell that gave the alarm and where the curfew is still sounded, is the first tower in the inner wall. It is most solidly built, and was strongly fortified, as it was expected to bear the brunt of an attack. In the Garden (or Bloody) Tower may still be seen the portcullis and its windlass. The dark circular stone staircase may be climbed to-day, and the scene of the murder of the little Princes pictured. Beside the Garden Tower is the well-known Wakefield Tower, which now contains the Regalia; its base is Norman work.

From the Wakefield Tower the visitor to-day crosses the site of the Palace, and has an almost entirely open view as he ascends towards the right-hand side of the Keep, which is entered on the north. The original entrance, however, was on the river side by an external staircase leading to the first floor. It is marked to-day by a very large window. This external stairway was in a small tower, which is to be seen in all the mediaeval drawings. In the 13th century a private spiral staircase was made from the Jewel House to St. John's Chapel. It was built in the thickness of the wall and the upper part is in use to-day; it was at the foot of the lower part that the bodies of the Princes murdered in 1483 were then buried; the bones, discovered there in 1647, were placed in a tomb in Westminster Abbey, and in 1933 experts reported that there was " reasonable probability that the traditional story was true."

Of the four towers of the Keep, three are square and the fourth circular. The apse of the Chapel of St. John, with its crypt, makes a semi-circular projection beyond the square formation of the Keep. The outer walls vary in thickness from 16 feet in the dungeons to 10 feet in the third floor, which has in the walls a triforium passage continuous with the triforium of the Chapel. This Chapel is the oldest and most perfectly preserved Norman Church in England. It has twelve pillars with five varieties of capital.

On the north the Postern Gate of the City wall is shown, together with a portion of the wall, and the City ditch. John Stow states that in 1078, King William, " having taken downe the Second Bulwarke in the east part of the wall from the Thames, builded this Tower," since called the White Tower, or the Keep, so that its eastern and southern defences were the old Roman wall. In 1190 the moat was begun and the " outward wall," enclosing ground taken from the City and East Smithfield, " besides breaking downe of the Citie wall from the White Tower to the first gate of the Citie, called the Posterne "; the second and outer lines of fortification were completed by Henry III. A fragment of the City wall is still to be seen by the S.E. angle of the Keep, beside the ruin of the Wardrobe Tower. In all probability the Wardrobe, Lanthorn, Wakefield and Bell Towers were erected on bastions or bulwarks of the Roman wall. William the Conqueror saw little else than the Keep, and it was left to others, principally Henry III, to complete the Tower of London, making it a palace as well as a fortress. The Keep as seen to-day is much as it was in Norman days, except for its windows; those on the first story were enlarged in the 17th century and those on the second and third stories in the 18th century.

The great Palace of the Tower was situated to the south and east of the Keep. It was bounded on the west by a wall, a considerable portion of which may be seen to-day; the roadway beside the wall led from the Garden Tower towards the Keep, and close to the latter was the gateway called Cold Harbour, which gave admittance to the Court of the Palace. To the right of the gateway and in front of the Keep was the Jewel House. On the opposite side of the courtyard was the Great Hall, erected by Henry III.

This Hall is shown in the drawing of 1597 (see Plate 1) as "decayed." On the right-hand side of the court will be seen a series of buildings called the Queen's Lodgings, and an archway will be noticed giving access to the second court, or Privy Court, of the Palace. This court formed an irregular quadrangle with a tower at each corner. The two on the north side were called the Wardrobe Tower (close to the Keep and shown in Plate 2 as circular in plan), a small portion of which may be seen to-day, and the Broad-arrow Tower (semi-circular in plan), which still exists. Between these was a range of buildings called The Wardrobe. The inner wall connected the Broad-arrow Tower with the Salt Tower, which was circular in plan, and there was a gallery or row of buildings within the wall between them. The Salt Tower is the only existing tower which may possibly be regarded as a portion of the old Palace, though it does not appear to have contained any of the apartments of the royal residence. The inner wall was carried straight on to the Well Tower, where it joined the outer wall. A building called the Queen's Gallery, which appears to have been partly of wood, or post-and-panel work, went in an oblique direction (as will be seen) from the Salt Tower to the Lanthorn Tower (since rebuilt). Another building, called the King's Gallery, extended from the Lanthorn Tower to the outer wall, which, with the walls and buildings previously mentioned, enclosed a triangular court planted as a garden, and called the Privy Garden. In order to make up for the absence of the inner wall, in this part of the Palace the outer wall was defended by two extra towers, the Cradle Tower and another, the Well Tower, which is described as " adjoining the King's Privy Closet." It is generally held that the Palace was demolished by Cromwell's order.

The Chapel of St. Peter and Vincula (appearing to the left of the Keep) was founded by Edward I, though, as will be seen, the present building is Tudor. As Macaulay says, " In truth, there is no sadder spot on earth than this little cemetery." Within the Communion rails lie buried the bodies of ten men and five women, all of whom played important parts in history during the 16th century. With the exception of one whose end was due to poison, and another who died a prisoner, all were executed within the Tower or upon Tower Hill. The women included two queens and Lady Jane Grey. The site of the scaffold is marked near the entrance to the Chapel. There is a Church in Rome with a similar name, and in it the " Chains of St. Peter " are exhibited once a year. The Beauchamp Tower forms part of the inner wall, and in it are to be seen the inscriptions carved by the unfortunate persons imprisoned there.

III.　Old London Bridge

In the foreground of Plate 5, of Old London Bridge, stands the church of St. Mary Overy, or, as we now know it, the Cathedral of St. Saviour, Southwark. In days before a bridge existed, a ferry plied across the river between Dowgate and the south bank; and a legend tells that the ferryman, a miser, made a fortune, which he left to his daughter. She, on the death of her lover, founded a convent at the south end of the ferry, where, having retired from the world, she ended her days. This convent became the great Augustinian Priory of St. Mary Overy; its chapel, built in the 13th century, was converted into a Parish Church in 1540, but little remains of it in the present

Church of St. Saviour. On the left of the Monastery is a portion of the Bishop of Winchester's London house. A rose window some 15 ft. in diameter is perhaps all that is left of the Palace. This was discovered, as a result of enemy action in 1940/41, incorporated into the wall of a commercial building. The dock which is seen in the illustration is the present St. Mary Overy Dock, and is the point from which the ferry was worked.

Old London Bridge was commenced in 1176 and finished about 30 years later; the architect, or founder, was a parish priest known by the name of Peter of Colechurch. St. Mary Colechurch stood in Cheapside at the corner of Old Jewry, but it was destroyed in the Great Fire, and not rebuilt. As Thomas à Becket was baptised in this Church, Peter Colechurch dedicated the chapel which he built on his bridge to England's youngest saint. Colechurch was buried in the chapel in 1205, and when the bridge was pulled down in 1832 his coffin was found in the foundations of the crypt; but, unfortunately, this was considered of no consequence, and his bones were thrown into the river.

The bridge was doubly fortified at the south end, while at the City entrance there was a single gateway. Houses soon began to be erected upon the bridge, and in 1460 there were 129, but, as changes and alterations were frequent owing to fire and tempest, it is difficult to say exactly what buildings were standing at any particular time. Brewer very naturally selected the most interesting date for his bridge, and gave himself artist's licence where he thought it desirable. It is probable that the chapel was not on the central pier, and it is more than likely that the original building had been destroyed prior to 1600, which is the date assigned by Brewer to his drawing; but the other most interesting buildings on it were erected only towards the close of the 16th century.

The Chapel of St. Thomas à Becket had an upper floor level with the street and a crypt, which was reached by a spiral staircase or from the water. It was a particularly beautiful structure; the upper chapel contained groups of elegant clustered columns and was lighted by pointed arch windows, but the crypt, though smaller, far exceeded it in beauty. The eastern extremity of both chapels was semi-hexagonal in plan.

In 1577, Nonesuch House took the place of the original Traitors' Gate; the south end of the bridge then became the Traitors' Gate, and the heads and limbs of those who had forfeited their lives were displayed upon it, as will be seen in the illustration. Nonesuch House was a timber building, supported by wooden struts from the piers. Drawings of it show that it was much like houses standing to-day in Hildesheim, in Germany; it is thought to have been brought from the Low Countries, and that the timber was floated up the Thames. It is not quite clear for what object it was built, but probably it was used as the Lord Mayor's residence. Sir John Hewitt, a Lord Mayor in Queen Elizabeth's reign, lived on the bridge, and there is an interesting incident recorded concerning his little daughter and his apprentice, named Edward Osborne. She was in the charge of a maid, who was playing with her at the window, when the child fell into the water. Osborne saw the accident, and without hesitation leapt from the window into the torrent and saved her. When the daughter grew up and her hand was sought by many eminent men, Sir John always said, " No, Osborne saved her, and Osborne shall enjoy her." Osborne did marry her and left a very large estate.

The foundations of the bridge were formed by driving piles into the mud and erecting within them the stone piers, which were protected by the wooden sterlings, seen uncovered in the drawing, because it represents low tide. The second arch on the City end of the old bridge was laid bare in 1921, when some of the piles were drawn up from the bed in which they had lain for hundreds of years. The first arch, also discovered, has been allowed to remain beneath the roadway. The present London Bridge, which was erected 100 feet to the west of the old one (1824/31), was also built on wooden piles driven into the mud, but its timber toes are encased in concrete. The waste of marshland, seen in Plate 3, was frequently covered with water, due to the holding up of the river by the nineteen wooden platforms or sterlings, for although the distance from one bank to the other was nearly 1,000 feet, there was only a waterway of some 200 feet. The spaces between the sterlings were called locks, and varied in width from 8 to 19 feet; at spring tides low water was some 6 feet below the level of the sterlings and mud shoals appeared near them. " The Fall," as it was called, was equally great at the return of the tide, so that large boats could get through safely only during some few hours at high water. Though the Thames watermen were experts at " Shooting the bridge," as it was called, without upsetting their boats, it was quite usual for passengers to land at " The Three Cranes," in Upper Thames Street, allow the boat to " shoot the bridge," and then re-enter it at Billingsgate.

There was a drawbridge in order that sailing boats coming up the river could pass above bridge, just as Tower Bridge to-day raises its bascules to allow ships with masts to enter the upper basin. The house on the other side of the drawbridge, next to Traitors' Gate, was erected at the same time as Nonesuch House, in 1577. It had semi-circular bow windows and a battlemented roof, and was probably the Bridge House, in which the business of the bridge and its estates was transacted. There was another house known by this name near the south end of the bridge, but this was used as a repair depot.

On the City end of the bridge there were houses and shops, but as it was only 20 feet wide, with 15 feet between the houses, they had to overhang the river. Later they were replaced by ordinary-looking houses, which were cleared away in 1758, when the bridge was widened to 45 feet. The Water Tower and the water-wheel (the former above and the latter below the platform seen in the drawing projecting over the river) were built by Peter Morris, the Dutchman, in 1582. He conceived the idea of supplying the City with water from the Thames by means of the water-wheel; he raised the water to the tower of St. Magnus-the-Martyr Church (seen more clearly in Plate 3, close to the bridge), and was thus able to supply water to a considerable portion of the City. During the Great Fire, the church was one of the first to be consumed; one-third of the houses on the bridge were burnt; and the water supply, which might have saved the City, was cut off. In later years four, if not five, wheels creaked and groaned before the arches, of which one was the Mill Lock Arch discovered in 1921. The Water Works were removed in 1822.

The approach to old London Bridge was from Gracechurch Street down Fish Street Hill, which was steeper, narrower, and, of course, very much rougher than at present. The footway passed under the present tower of the Church of St. Magnus-the-Martyr.

IV. Old St. Paul's

OLD St. Paul's was built from 1085 to 1155, and replaced the Church erected by Ethelbert, King of Kent, in 607, which was burnt down during The Conqueror's reign. An old historian records, " So stately and beautiful was it, that it was worthily numbered among the most famous buildings." The Norman apse of the Cathedral was replaced by an Early English choir, which was commenced in 1221; the eight eastern bays were built from 1255 to 1283 and the whole was subsequently referred to as the " New Work." It included a beautiful rose window enclosed in a square, beneath which were seven large and very wide lights. The flying buttresses of the " New Work " and of the transepts will be noted, and also those at the base of the beautiful spire. This spire was of wood, covered with lead; it was destroyed by fire in 1561, owing to the carelessness of a plumber, and was never rebuilt. The Cathedral itself was left a ruin by the Great Fire in 1666. Its noble length, the solemn Norman of its nave, the developed and rich Gothic of its choir and the majesty of proportion with which the English system of a square east end was carried out, must have made it more like Ely Cathedral than any other of our great churches, but the spire resembled most that of Norwich Cathedral. The spire rose to the height of no less than 520 feet. (Plate 6.)

The Clochier or bell-tower (A) stood near the east end, apart from the Cathedral; it was a square stone tower crowned with a wooden spire, on the summit of which was a gilded statue of St. Paul. In the tower were hung four bells, called the " Jesus Bells " because they came from the chapel of that name in the crypt of the Cathedral. It is recorded that Henry VIII lost both the statue and the bells at one throw of the dice to Sir Miles Partridge; in the following reign Sir Miles lost his head. The crypt also contained the Parish Church, called St. Faith's. When the Guild which met in the Jesus' Chapel was dissolved, the chapel was united to St. Faith's. In the present Cathedral there is a Jesus' Chapel at the east end and a St. Faith's in the crypt.

Paul's Cross (B), in the foreground, was a place of preaching for some 250 years. When the King came to hear the preaching, he occupied what was called the King's Closet (C), an erection near the Cathedral itself. The " Shrowds " (D) or cloisters are seen adjacent to the choir and north transept. Over the north portion of the " Shrowds " was the Consistory Court (E). Shiryngton's Chapel (F) is just to the right of the north transept entrance; and Shiryngton's Library (G) is next to the chapel. Above the chapel may be seen the Bell-tower (J), and also Pardon Church (H); the " Hawgh " or graveyard was surrounded by cloisters, upon the walls of which was the remarkable painting, the " Dance of Death," depicting Death requiring old and young, rich and poor, to join in the universal " dance." The building in the foreground on the right (K) was a mortuary chapel called " The Charnell." The buildings on the north-west of the Cathedral precincts may also be seen in Plate 10.

Old St. Paul's exceeded 600 feet in length and was considerably longer than the present Cathedral. The nave was 300 feet long and had 12 bays; while the choir was its equal in length with the same number of bays. This arrangement was unique, and the perspective of the interior must have been exceptionally fine. Brewer made three drawings of the interior as a result of his research (see Plates 7, 8, and 9). Hollar's drawings, made before the Cathedral's destruction, were the basis for Brewer's pictures. The nave was known as Paul's Walk. There was a flight of steps giving entrance to the choir, beyond which was the remainder of the " New Work." In the crypt of the present Cathedral there are seven mutilated effigies, and a small tablet to the memory of Sir Simon Baskervile (to be seen in Plate 9), on the first pillar on the left). Next beyond this pillar is the Chantry Chapel of John of Gaunt, Duke of Lancaster (d. 1399). Apart from these effigies and the tablet, only one effigy escaped the Great Fire, and it has been restored to a place in the south aisle of the present choir. It is that of John Donne, Dean of St. Paul's, who died only thirty-five years before the Fire. The monument, which it is said was designed by himself, stood erect until the roof had fallen through the floor, when it somehow slipped into the crypt unharmed.

Plate 6 includes Paul's Cross in what was the Great Cemetery, and its site to-day is marked near the Cross erected in 1910, from the design of the late Sir Reginald Blomfield, R.A. The entrance to the Churchyard from Cheapside will be noticed, and there were gateways at the south-east and on the south and west. From the drawing of Ludgate, Plate 11, it will be observed that the Chapter House with cloisters was on the south. In the churchyard of to-day, part of the foundations of the Chapter House and of the cloisters, including the pavement, may still be seen. It was the only Cathedral in England which had cloisters on both sides of the nave. Brewer believed that at the west end the Cathedral had a Galilee porch, which will be seen in Plate 11, and he has recorded very good reasons for his opinion. It was not until 1625 that Inigo Jones built his classical portico to the Cathedral, which disappeared with Wren's rebuilding. The Parish Church of St. Gregory-by-St. Paul's (on the right of the west end of the Cathedral), the Bishop's Palace and the Deanery may all be noted in Plate 11. The residence of the Bishop was removed to Aldersgate Street before the Great Fire, but the Deanery is still at the south-west corner of the Churchyard, in Dean's Court.

V. Cheapside

CHEAPSIDE, in the days of Henry VIII, covered very much the same ground that it does to-day; it was also about the same width, though it broadened out towards the west, where the centre of the street was occupied by St. Michael's Church. In front of the Church was a fountain, called the Lesser Conduit, a square building with octagonal pinnacles at the angles. To the right of this, in Plate 10, will be seen the Church of St. Peter Cheap, which had a fairly lofty western tower, crowned by a small domical turret of wood. Not a single building in Cheapside escaped the Fire; and a letter written at the time states, " You may stand where Cheapside was and see the Thames." At the corner of Wood Street, in Cheapside, the great plane tree, with which all Londoners are familiar, overhangs the Churchyard of St. Peter Cheap, and also three little shops each of two rooms only. These shops were built directly after the Fire, on the site of what had been called " The Longe Shoppe."

In the centre of the road, and not far from the Church of St. Peter Cheap, stood the High Cross of Cheap, a remarkably beautiful structure. It was one of the Eleanor Crosses, erected by Edward I, who set up one at each place on which his wife's body rested on its way to Westminster. The last Cross was at the village of Charing, hence Charing Cross.

On the south side, between Bread Street and Bow Church, stood a magnificent timber building, known as Goldsmith's Row. It consisted of a series of houses and shops, four stories high, and with ten gables all alike. It was richly ornamented with carvings of woodmen mounted on " monstrous beasts," and decorated with coats of arms in colour and gilt. The " Row " was built by Thomas Wood, the goldsmith in 1491, when Cheapside was the goldsmith's quarter. Next to it is the Church of St. Mary-le-Bow. As to-day, except for the tower, it did not flank Cheapside. The tower had an interesting clock upon it, and a very beautiful arched summit with five open lanterns. The term " Bow Church " may be due to the arches of the tower, or to those of the crypt. John Stow says: " This Church in the reigne of William Conquerour, being in this Citie builded on Arches of Stone, was therefore called newe Marie Church, of Saint Marie de Arcubus, or, le Bow in West Cheaping. As Stratford Bridge being the first, builded (by Matilde the Queene, wife of Henrie the first) with Arches of Stone, was called Stratford le Bow, which names to the said Church and Bridge remayneth till this day."

Bow Church was one of thirteen churches within the City which were called " peculiars," because they did not belong to the diocese of London, but to that of Canterbury. The Court of Arches was the Archbishop's Court, and in Bow Church the " confirmation " of the election of Bishops took place. The Norman crypt (1070) escaped the Great Fire; this and the tower, which is one of Wren's masterpieces, survived the enemy action that destroyed all but the walls of the Church in 1940/41. The tower has had to be rebuilt.

In front of Bow Church was a costly building of stone, known as the " Crown Sild," or " Sildam," with an open arcade in the upper story facing the street, which was used by Royalty and their visitors for witnessing tournaments, pageants, and processions. The tower of the present church has a balcony overlooking the street, placed there by Wren to commemorate the " Crown Sild." In the foreground, in the centre of the street, stood the upper conduit, " The Standard." It was an octagonal tower crowned by a projecting parapet and lantern, all of stone. As the houses had no water supply, the inhabitants were largely dependent upon such fountains. Except for a central gulley in such a wide thoroughfare as this, the streets were not drained even for surface water, and the houses had no drainage system. Water spouts discharged their contents upon the passers-by in the streets, and receptacles were emptied from the windows. We may presume that most of the water found its way to the river sooner or later! There was a third fountain in Cheapside at the east end (just out of the picture) called the Great Conduit.

In the foreground of the illustration on the right is shown a remarkable house all of timber, probably an inn or hostelry. It had a great hipped roof and two projecting oriels at the angles, which extended outwards as they increased in height.

On referring to Plate 4 it will be seen that Cheapside was practically the centre of the City. To-day the central point is farther east, where the Bank of England, the Royal Exchange and the Mansion House face one another. Between this point and Cheapside, with which it is in line, still lies the thoroughfare called Poultry. At the east end of Poultry stood St. Mildred's Church, whose site to-day is marked by St. Mildred Court. The Bank of England occupies the site of the parish and Church of St. Christopher-le-Stocks, so called because in front of this Church stood the Lord Mayor's stocks, in which wrong-doers were imprisoned by their arms or legs. The graveyard became the Fountain Court of the Bank. On the site of the Lord Mayor's residence, the Mansion House, there stood, until nearly half-way through the 18th century, the Stocks Market, in which fish and meat were offered for sale at stalls and shambles. Behind it was the Church of St. Mary Woolchurch, which was not rebuilt after the Great Fire, and the Market was extended to occupy its site. A conduit, or fountain, may be seen in Plate 4 standing at this end of the thoroughfare, near where the statue of Wellington is to-day. The Royal Exchange was not founded till Elizabeth's reign, when it faced Cornhill, and the west front was blocked up by houses; it was destroyed in the Great Fire of 1666; the statue of its founder, Gresham, alone was spared.

The name Cheapside is from the Anglo-Saxon *ceap*—to buy—and it is interesting to note the names of the adjoining streets, all of which survive to tell of the goods sold in them in days gone by; thus, Bread Street, Milk Street, Poultry, Honey Lane Market, Friday Street (for fish), and Ironmonger Lane. In Bucklersbury lived the druggists and apothecaries. Cheapside was also called the Westcheap, and there is an Eastcheap in the eastern portion of the City. Queen Street and King Street, forming a direct approach to the Guildhall by crossing Cheapside, were the only new thoroughfares made by Wren after the Great Fire, though some were widened.

Old St. Paul's Cathedral, which occupies such a central position in this picture, is fully described with Plate 6. Facing this (the east) end of the Cathedral, stood St. Paul's School, which was founded by Dean Colet in 1509. It was destroyed by the Great Fire; only the bust of the Founder was saved, and it is preserved in the present School, which migrated to West London in 1884.

A portion of Baynard's Castle appears to the left of Bow Church tower. It was in Baynard's Castle that Richard, Duke of Gloucester, was offered and accepted the Crown, and it was probably there that he, as Richard III, plotted the murder of his nephews, of whom one was the young King Edward V; this deed was carried out in the Bloody Tower two months later.

VI. Ludgate

In Plate 11, Brewer shows Old St. Paul's from the west. It will be noticed that half-way up Ludgate Hill stands Lud Gate, while at the top of the hill there is another gateway, which was the entrance to the West Churchyard. On one side of the entrance was Creed Lane, and in days of old the monks started their processionals about the Cathedral from here by reciting the Creed. They said the " Ave Maria " in Ave Maria Lane and the " Pater Noster " in Paternoster Row, and concluded their prayers at Amen Corner. Of this we are reminded by the streets still bearing those names. Other gateways giving access to the Churchyard may be seen from Cheapside, by St. Austin's Gate (just to the right of the Clochier), and from the south by a gateway called Paul's Chain. The two Cathedral entrances from Paternoster Row were by Canon Alley and Paul's Alley, and these passages bear the same names to-day.

The Church with the tall square tower in the foreground on the right of Plate 11 is St. Bride's. In front of it in Fleet Street was a large fountain called the Old Conduit, crowned by a statue of St. Christopher, standing upon a tower. Within the tower of the fountain were chimes of bells " worked by machinery " which was, presumably, set in motion by water-power.

Opposite the Church stood a mansion called the Old Bourne Hall, taking its name from the Old Bourne River (hence Holborn), which was a tributary of the Fleet River; another derivation for Holborn is " Hollow Bourne." The Fleet and the bridge over it are clearly seen in the illustration. It now runs underground and discharges into the Thames under Blackfriars railway bridge. Brewer represents the City ditch passing Ludgate and joining the Fleet just below the Fleet Bridge, but he must have been mistaken in thus completing the circuit of the City ditch, for there is no evidence of the existence of the ditch on the west side of the City, and the contours exclude the possibility of such a waterway. This Plate gives a good representation of the mean character of most of the dwellings, and even suggests the squalor which is known to have been so prevalent.

Lud Gate is said to have been founded by " Lud," an early King of Britain. " The Cronycullys of Englonde " tells us " he lete make a fayre gate and called hit Lud Gate after his name." But the gate in the illustration is not the original; it was built about 1450 by a man named Foster, who at one time was lodged in the Debtors' Prison over the gate, but eventually became Sir Stephen Foster, Lord Mayor of London. He rebuilt Lud Gate and the Debtors' Prison, and, remembering his own sufferings, abolished the practice of making the helpless debtors pay for water and lodging. In Queen Elizabeth's reign Lud Gate was rebuilt, and upon it were placed statues of King Lud and Her Majesty. That of Queen Bess may be seen to-day over one of the entrances to the Church of St. Dunstan-in-the-West, Fleet Street.

On Ludgate Hill, to the left of the Gate, will be seen the stone tower of St. Martin's Church, which projected out into the roadway; to-day its successor is flush with the houses of the street, and part of its western wall is said to rest upon the foundations of the City wall. When Wren was clearing the ground for new foundations after the Great Fire he came upon a Roman sepulchral stone (to be seen in Oxford) bearing the figure of a soldier grasping a sword in one hand. The inscription upon it has been translated thus: " To the departed spirits. TO VIVIUS MARCIANUS, soldier of the Second Augustan Legion. JANUARIA MARTINA, his dutiful wife, raised this memorial." Many such stones were used by the Romans as material for their wall.

The Hall of the Worshipful Company of Stationers stands behind the Church, and in the Company's garden, which may be seen to-day between them, heretical books were burnt in the days when the patron of the Company, the Archbishop of Canterbury, exercised a very real censorship over every book that was printed. In the garden and also in Amen Court the modern wall built on the foundations of the ancient wall may be seen. Stationers' Hall, rebuilt after the Great Fire, stands on the edge of a vast area devastated by incendiaries in 1940/41; it was attacked by fire from four directions and lost its roof. The Hall has now been restored.

The large block of buildings on the right of Lud Gate is the Monastery of the Dominicans, or Black Friars, which included a considerable area of ground within walls and gates; it contained also the Chapel of St. Anne, which is shown as having a slender square tower. After the Dissolution, the Church occupied the site of the cloisters where Brewer shows it, but St. Anne's Chapel was originally on the south side of the Monastery. The Monastery was free of the City, and so large was it that Parliament frequently met there. In the Great Hall the divorce proceedings of Queen Catherine of Aragon took place. The passage now called Church Entry, which has the churchyard of St. Anne on its right, marks the east wall of the cloisters where the black-cowled monks paced up and down, and the first portion of the passage marks the aisle beneath the steeple which divided the preaching nave from the choir of the Monastery.

Just beyond Church Entry passage is Playhouse Yard of to-day. After the Dissolution of the Monastery part of it was used for the storage of properties for pageants; and Shakespeare and his friends built their first playhouse there. In that theatre they re-enacted in the play *Henry VIII* the very scene that had taken place in the Great Hall of the Monastery: the Trial of Catherine of Aragon. Remains of the Great Hall were discovered when *The Times* printing office was rebuilt on part of the site. The Hall of the Apothecaries' Company occupies the site of the Guest Hall.

The Church of St. Andrew-by-the-Wardrobe (seen in the Plate above the Monastery tower) takes its description from the King's Great Wardrobe, a mansion used as an office for the keepers of the royal apparel, standing to the north of the Church where Wardrobe Place is now. The Church, built by Wren after the Fire on the same site, occupied a commanding position in Queen Victoria Street, but enemy action in 1940/41 left only its walls.

On the river-side may be noted, from right to left, part of Baynard's Castle, St. Mary Somerset Church (which was destroyed in the Fire; Wren's tower only now remains), Queenhithe (the one harbour above bridge), and beyond it the Steelyard. In 1266 merchants from Hamburg established a branch of the Hanseatic League in what became known as the Steelyard. The German merchants were called " Easter-lings," and their gold was of such good value that it was known as " sterling," and hence became a standard adopted for English currency. In 1852 the warehouses were sold and Cannon Street Station was built over the site and Steelyard Lane.

On the sky-line may be noted from left to right, Bow Church, the Clochier to the right of the Cathedral, the lofty spire of St. Laurence Pountney, London Bridge, the Tower of London, and the Church of St. Mary Overy, now known as St. Saviour's, Southwark.

Beyond the Black Friars' Monastery (going westward) was Bridewell Palace, of which the site is still marked by Bridewell Place, and then came the Monastery of the Carmelites or White Friars, which, as may be seen in Plate 3, had a conspicuous tower. It was destroyed at the Dissolution. The street leading to-day from Fleet Street to the site of their House is called Whitefriars Street.

VII. 𝔑𝔢𝔴𝔤𝔞𝔱𝔢

THE gateway called Newgate, shown in the foreground on the right in Plate 12, was rebuilt by or at the expense of Richard Whittington, the famous Lord Mayor of London, who also built Newgate Prison and a library for the Grey Friars. The City wall is also to be seen in the foreground, and in front of it the tower of St. Sepulchre's Church, which stands to-day in Holborn. The Church was partially destroyed in the Great Fire, but the tower and porch with its fan vaulting survived. Newgate Prison is just out of the picture; it was built upon the City wall to the right of the gateway.

Beyond Newgate, within the City the first part of the street which is now known as Newgate Street was called Blow Bladder Street, and then came The Shambles and Newgate Market. Stinking Lane was the former name for King Edward Street. As the names imply, the quarter was not a savoury one, and, as will be seen in the illustration, along the middle of the " thoroughfare " stood the butchers' stalls; it also contained the City Shambles. The Church half-way up on the left-hand side was called St. Nicholas Shambles. On the other side was the Church of St. Ewin, and behind a line of houses may be seen the garden of the Bishop of London's Palace.

The great building in the centre of the view is the Church of the Monastery of the Franciscans, or Grey Friars, an Order pledged to poverty, and such was their popularity that with the gifts they received they built up the largest Church in the whole City after St. Paul's. It had a vast nave and aisles, while the choir with aisles was of the same width as the nave; the length of the Church was 311 feet. In front of the west entrance is to be seen the outer court, with the library on the left of it; beyond are the cloisters and monastic buildings. The dormitory is over the north cloister, and the Infirmary with its Chapel is behind the east cloister. The building of the Church was commenced in 1306.

The Monastery fared rather better than some others at the Dissolution, for fifteen years after it Edward VI founded Christ's Hospital, and devoted the best part of the Monastery to his school for poor boys. The choir of the Church was converted into a Parish Church, and joined with St. Nicholas. It was known as Christ Church, and covered the site of the present church of that name in Newgate Street and the graveyard opposite to it. The Church and the School were burnt down in the Great Fire, and the School, which was also known as the Blue Coat School, was in 1902 removed to Horsham. Of Wren's Christ Church, the tower and walls only survived enemy action in 1940/41.

Other buildings to be seen in the distance are Bow Church, in Cheapside, and also another Church bearing a familiar name, St. Martin's-le-Grand, on the site subsequently occupied by the old General Post Office. It appears in the illustration above the farther end of St. Nicholas Shambles. St. Martin's-le-Grand was a sanctuary and collegiate Church, and, as within the " Cities of Refuge," anyone guilty of a crime found there safety and freedom from arrest, a privilege which was discontinued after the Dissolution of the Monasteries. It was one of the very oldest religious foundations, dating from Saxon times, and later, under the Normans, it was from its belfry that the curfew (*couvre le feu*) first sounded, giving the warning, which was taken up by the other churches, that all lights and fires must be extinguished and the gates of the City closed for the night.

The wall of the City, which is seen in the foreground, will be noticed again, with the City ditch, in the middle distance, for it made a right-angle turn a few yards north of Newgate. When the Blue Coat School was pulled down and the site cleared for the King Edward Post Office yard, an almost complete bastion of the City wall was discovered. It might well be the one which is on the left-hand edge of the picture, and to-day it may be seen in the middle of the mail van yard. The next portions of wall are to be found in the graveyards of St. Botolph's Without, Aldersgate, and St. Giles's, Cripplegate, and another portion between them has been laid bare as a result of enemy action in 1940/41. The Church of St. Giles was of considerable interest as being John Milton's Church; standing outside the City wall it escaped the Great Fire, but it did not escape the fire from enemy action. It has now been completely restored under the direction of Messrs. W. Godfrey Allen, M.A., F.S.A., F.R.I.B.A., and the late Gilbert P. Meaden, F.S.A. The wall, which ran nearly north from near Aldersgate to Cripple-

24

gate, there took another right-angle turn, and in the Churchyards of St. Alphage and of All Hallows-on-the-Wall, both in the street called London Wall, there are remains of the wall to be seen. There are several portions of the east wall. The one within the Tower has already been mentioned. Of the others in order going north, the first may be found easily and examined closely at the end of a yard called Trinity Place. In Cooper's Row, near by, the warehouse of Messrs. Joseph Barber & Co., Ltd., contains the most complete portion of the ancient wall. In the basement may be seen the Roman masonry, said to date from about A.D. 120; on the ground floor is the mediaeval portion with a loop-hole window; and on the first floor there is a sentry-walk and a breast-high portion of the 15th century wall. It is some 13 feet below the present surface of the City that Roman work can be seen. The foundations of No. 1 Crutched Friars also contain a piece of the wall in very good condition. There is one other similar portion to be seen at No. 41 Ludgate Hill. On reference to Plate 11, it will be noted that from Ludgate the wall was deflected in order to enclose the Monastery of the Black Friars, who obtained permission from Edward I for this to be done. Originally, the City had a south wall, which ran parallel with Thames Street and had two gates, Dowgate and Billingsgate, above and below London Bridge respectively, but it disappeared during the twelfth century, except for that portion which forms part of the south wall of the Tower of London. There was, however, one other south gate, the one at the City end of London Bridge.

The seven gates, Aldgate on the east, Bishopsgate, Moorgate, Cripplegate and Aldersgate on the north, and Newgate and Ludgate on the west, were closed at sunset daily until the year 1760, when they were pulled down, and the City wall gradually disappeared with the exception of the fragments mentioned above. The stones of the City gates were used to support the piers and sterlings of Old London Bridge. Postern Row, marking the site of the Postern Gate on Tower Hill, was cleared away in 1882. There was also a postern gate between Moorgate and Cripplegate, called Aldermanbury Postern, and its site is marked by the short street of that name. Moorgate was originally only a postern in the City Wall, but in 1415 the little gate was pulled down and a larger one built to the westward of it.

The City ditch was supplied with water from the Moorfields, not from the River Thames as shown by Brewer in Plate 3. The Moorfields were finally drained in 1606, but during Elizabeth's reign the City ditch was filled up, as it had become offensive. During the 16th century the Moor was made a playground for London, where archery and other sports were practised. A portion of it, belonging to the Honourable Artillery Company, is still used for gunnery and sports.

VIII. Aldgate

ALDGATE, whether approached from the east or from within the City, may have reminded many of the proverbial "Needle's Eye." From Whitechapel there was a broad road, ending at St. Botolph's Church, with its three naves of equal height and width, and its fine tower with flying buttresses supporting its final turret; the bridge over the City ditch had then to be crossed. But the gateway with its four towers, on which were displayed the heads of traitors, did not face east, but north; so that a traveller had to take a sharp turn left in order to pass through it, and then another turn to the right through the gateway of the Priory of Holy Trinity, also called Christ Church. The peculiar position of the City gate, which belonged to the Priory, was due to the fact that it was erected by the monks with a view to their own convenience.

Leadenhall Street is on the right of Plate 13, and a pedestrian passing down the street reached a gateway leading into the same courtyard of the Priory. Approached from Fenchurch Street a similar gateway, just seen on the right of the other, also gave access to the courtyard. It was a constant source of controversy between the fraternity and the civilian population whether or not there was a right of way through the courtyard. There was an alternative route, but it was very circuitous, by a narrow lane, called Poor Jewry, which wound round by the City wall and so led out of the City gate. The thoroughfare is now known as Jewry Street.

The tower of the Church of St. Andrew Undershaft, in Leadenhall Street, appears in the right-hand corner of the illustration. On May Day it was the custom to erect in front of it a maypole so high that it overtopped the steeple of the Church, which thus received the name of Undershaft. In Edward VI's reign the shaft was destroyed as a relic of idolatry. The Church contains a monument to one who lived in the 16th century and was for us an important person, John Stow, the great antiquary and topographer. It is to him we are indebted for most valuable information concerning mediaeval London, but his own generation did not appreciate his labours, and in his declining years the poor man had to ask James I for permission to beg. Beside the Church is the street called St. Mary Axe, in which there stood formerly a church dedicated to St. Mary the Virgin, St. Ursula and the Eleven Thousand Virgins, and called St. Mary-at-Axe, from an axe being the sign of an adjacent house. As will be seen in Plate 13, a short distance from St. Andrew Undershaft is the Church of St. Katherine Cree, or Christ Church. Both these churches escaped the Fire, but neither building is very old. The origin of the latter Church is interesting. The parishioners used to worship in the Priory itself, but this practice being found inconvenient there was built for them, about the year 1300, this Church, which received the second or alternative name of the Priory. The Church was rebuilt in 1630, when the cloister shown in the picture on the left of the west entrance was pulled down, and its site included in that of the new Church. The tower is almost entirely that of the earlier Church, and access to-day is gained by a south doorway under it. Immediately within it there were seven steps leading down to the floor of the Church, and one of the original pillars near the tower may be seen to-day with its capital only a few feet above the level of the present nave.

The Priory of the Holy Trinity was founded by Matilda, Queen of Henry I, about the year 1108, for the regular Canons of the Order of St. Augustine, and it became the wealthiest in the City. It was surrounded by four courtyards. The principal entrance was from Leadenhall Street, beside Cree Church, and along the Cree Lane of to-day. The large and small arches of the entrance are to be seen in the Plate. Here was the Great Hall; beyond it was the doorway leading to the Cloisters, and then came the great west entrance of this magnificent Priory Church. The building was similar in construction to St. Saviour's, Southwark, as we now know it; but the Priory had some very fine chapels at the east end, and beautiful cloisters. Brewer shows the cloisters on the south, but they were on the north on the site of what we know as Mitre Square. Between the cloisters and Leadenhall Street may be seen in the drawing the cemetery of Cree Church.

26

In the east courtyard, through which the traffic passed, there was the Aldgate Pump, still a familiar object, though it does not look so interesting as it did then. The Prior lived in the house near-by on the farther side of the courtyard. In the foreground on the left is the house of the Abbot of Bury St. Edmunds. Bury Street, which exists to-day, ran between the Abbot's house and the Priory. John Stow lived from 1547 to 1570 in a house facing the Aldgate Pump at the corner formed by Leadenhall Street and Fenchurch Street.

At the Dissolution, the Priory, which with the exception of Westminster was the finest in Middlesex, was given over to Sir Thomas Audley, who pulled it down and sold the materials for sixpence a cart-load. Sir Thomas first offered the great Church of the Priory to the parishioners of St. Katherine's in exchange for their small parish church, which he wanted to pull down so that he might " build there towards the street," but they refused the offer. The mansion which he built on the site of the Priory passed (through the marriage of his daughter) to the Duke of Norfolk; and Duke Street and Mitre Street of to-day alone remain to mark the site of the Priory. In 1622 a Church was built, called Trinity Christ's Church, and afterwards St. James's, Duke's Place, after James I, for the benefit of those inhabitants who had, since the demolition of the Priory, worshipped in St. Katherine Cree, but wanted a parish church of their own. St. James's was pulled down in 1874. It occupied the site of the Chapter House on the north-east of the Priory Church.

The Church of St. Botolph, Aldgate, has already been mentioned; it was founded in the reign of The Conqueror, and in 1115 was given to the Priors of Holy Trinity, by whom it was rebuilt. The present church is comparatively modern and, since the Church of Holy Trinity in the Minories has been closed, it has given a resting place to what is probably an interesting relic of Tower Hill executions. The story is told in " Unknown London " of how the reputed head of the Duke of Suffolk, father of Lady Jane Grey, has been preserved there and gives rise to curious speculations.

To the left of the massive tower of the Priory Church we may note the small tower and turret of the Church of St. Augustine-on-the-Wall and an ecclesiastical hospital, called " The Papey," attached to it; also the City wall and ditch, beyond which is the open country. The house, surrounded by its garden and wall, belonged to the Priory and was called " The Dove House "; between it and the City ditch was " Bevis Marks," which was probably a meat market, hence the name " Marks "; " Bevis " is from " beeves." The district is called Bevis Marks to this day. On the sky-line are (from left to right) Hackney Church, West Ham Church and Priory, Bow Church, Bromley Priory, and St. Mary's Church in Whitechapel Road.

IX. Ely Place

In the 16th century, London had extended beyond its walls, especially westward; and Brewer has depicted in Plate 14 " A Monastic Suburb," which existed to the north-west. The northern portion of the City appears on the sky-line to the right, and Aldersgate may be seen in the corner of the illustration. In the foreground on the right is Holborn, which was reached from Newgate Street after crossing the valley now spanned by Holborn Viaduct. Clerkenwell occupies the mid-left of the picture, and Ely Place is in the immediate foreground. Within this suburb there were no fewer than six monastic institutions, together with the Bishop of Ely's Palace and Chapel.

Just beyond and to the right of the open space, which is Smithfield, is the noble Priory Church of St. Bartholomew the Great. The west entrance is seen in the illustration and the doorway of the south aisle forms the gateway to-day, giving access to the churchyard which occupies the site of the nave. The present entrance to the Church is at the farther end of what was once the south aisle. When the Priory Church was surrendered in 1539 to Henry VIII, the nave, side-chapels and north transept were destroyed; the whole Priory was sold to Sir Richard Rich. It is, therefore, only the choir that remains intact, though the Lady Chapel, transepts, crypt, and part of the cloisters have been restored. From the four central piers, there are four bays on each side of the choir and seven smaller semi-circular arches form an apse, around which passes an ambulatory, while above is a triforium of the same character; all this is fine Norman work, except for the central piers of the apse and the triforium at the east end, which have been restored. The monument of the founder is in one of the choir bays, and is most striking. Rahere is represented as a monk with shaven tonsure in the robes of his Order, that of the Austin Canons, commonly called " Black Canons " from their black cloaks and hoods. It is the most interesting and structurally it is the oldest Parish Church, for such it has been since the Dissolution, in the whole of London.

Next on the right of St. Bartholomew the Great are the buildings of the Confraternity of the Holy Trinity, and in front of them is the Priory of St. Bartholomew the Less. The Great Fire of 1666 was arrested at Pye Corner only a few yards from the Priory, the tower of which still stands and forms part of the Chapel of St. Bartholomew's Hospital. The famous hospital, only a portion of which appears in the illustration, was built by Rahere, the Pilgrim, in gratitude to St. Bartholomew for restoring him to health. At the Saint's bidding he also founded the Church and Priory of St. Bartholomew the Great in 1123. The hospital has thus continued his beneficent work for over eight centuries.

To the left of Smithfield will be observed, first the entrance gateway and then the Church, with a spire, of the Military Priory of St. John of Jerusalem, in front of which a troop of horse is drawn up. The entrance gate, known as St. John's, Clerkenwell, still exists; it belongs to " The Grand Priory of the Order of the Hospital of St. John of Jerusalem in England," and is also the headquarters of the St. John Ambulance Association. The connection with Jerusalem is continued, as the Knights maintain a hospital there. The Church was consecrated in the year 1185 by Heraclius, the Patriarch of Jerusalem, and consisted of a circular nave, 65 feet in diameter, and a rectangular choir, but this Church was burnt by the Wat Tyler rebels in 1381. It was replaced by a rectangular nave with a choir; the latter forms the present Church, which was erected on the foundations of the old choir, as may be seen by inspecting them and the bases of the original piers. The circular nave has been traced in paving stones, and fragments of the foundations of it have been disclosed. The beautiful crypt, which is partly Norman and partly of later date, is full of interest.

On the left side of the illustration is another Priory, that of the Black Nuns, also known as the Priory of St. James, Clerkenwell. It became the Parish Church of that name at the Dissolution, but has been rebuilt since. Above St. John's Gate is to be seen the Charterhouse, the small Carthusian Monastery which included the Church of the Knights Hospitallers. At the Dissolution the Church was destroyed and the Charterhouse became private property; and in 1611 it was converted into a school for boys, which in 1872 was removed to Godalming.

The stream which is seen in the illustration was known as the River of Wells, as it was fed by numerous wells. Of these, Clerks' Wells (*i.e.*, Parish Clerks'), or Clerkenwell, and St. Bridget's or Bridewell, are familiar names. The stream lower down became the Fleet, which also received the Bourne. It must have been a pleasant place for a walk beside the stream, with its water-wheel, or by the elm trees and along the " smooth field," or Smithfield, before it became notorious as the place where " heretics " were burnt in the 16th century. Here Bartholomew Fair, with its revels, was held for many ages, and jousts, tournaments, revelries and fairs took place. The pond was known as the Horsepoole.

Ely Place or Palace, the London house of the Bishops of Ely since 1290, is in the immediate foreground. The Bishop's Chapel shown in the illustration may still be visited; it is now the Church of St. Etheldreda, a Roman Catholic establishment. It was in 1874 that Services in Communion with the Church of Rome were resumed in it and the building is unique in this respect. The external porch gives access to the upper chapel, and steps lead to the crypt beneath. A visit either to the upper chapel, to the crypt with its huge timber beams, or to the cloister (seen in Plate 14) beside the Church, will suggest, by its romantic atmosphere, a return to the Middle Ages. The Palace was the noblest ecclesiastical residence in London. Of the two courts, the first, entered from Holborn, contained the hall; while the second, with a cloister, adjoined the Chapel. The immense garden belonging to the Palace was the subject of a controversy between Queen Elizabeth and the Bishop of Ely, named Richard Cox, who was a very remarkable man. As one of the earliest of the Reformers, he had suffered for his faith, and had fled to the Continent. On his return he filled the See of Ely for 20 years. Elizabeth had as Lord Chancellor her favourite, Sir Christopher Hatton, who had obtained a lease of the gatehouse and other portions of the Palace and wanted part of the very large garden; but Bishop Cox saw no reason why any part of the diocesan property should be given up as desired, and wished to resign rather than yield to the Queen's demands. He died the following year (1581), and later on, after long disputes, Hatton's successor obtained possession of Hatton House, as it was then called, and the garden. As a result we now see the Hatton Garden of to-day, running parallel with Ely Place. The strawberries of Ely Place are alluded to in Shakespeare's play *Richard II, Act II;, Scene IV.*

> Richard, Duke of Gloucester, to the Bishop of Ely:
> My Lord of Ely, when I was last in Holborn,
> I saw good strawberries in your garden there:
> I do beseech you send for some of them.

The " Mitre " Inn, approached by the passage-way seen in the foreground of the picture, stood against the Palace residence, and its successor may be found to-day on the same spot bearing a stone sign, a mitre, with the date 1456.

X. Westminster

THE Palace of Westminster stands in the forefront of Plate 15, in which it is viewed from the east. Its origin cannot be clearly ascertained, and the first authentic notices of this vast historical edifice refer to the time of Edward the Confessor, who certainly made it his principal residence. He either built or rebuilt the Palace, which was both historically and structurally connected with the Abbey, which may be seen in the background of the illustration. William I is said to have added the building known as the " Court of Requests," and William Rufus erected Westminster Hall. These two halls are to be seen left and right of St. Stephen's Chapel, which stands in the centre of the illustration. Stephen has been credited with the foundation of the chapel, which bears the name of St. Stephen's; but Brewer considered that the original chapel was the work of Henry III.

In 1298 occurred one of those disastrous fires which have five times reduced the greater portion of the old Palace to ruins. St. Stephen's Chapel, which had been only just completed and decorated in a most costly manner, was entirely destroyed. Edward I commenced the building of its successor, but it was not until the reign of Edward III that even the " Lower Chapel " was completed; and the whole of the upper chapel was certainly the work of that monarch. The accounts for its building and decoration are still preserved, and form the most interesting series of documents of this kind in existence. With the exception of some of the statues everything, including the costly pictures painted upon the walls, was paid for by day wages. The originals of two of the pictures, viz., Mercury and Eustace, are in the British Museum, and reproductions of these and others are to be seen in the Houses of Parliament. The names of the master masons, the painters, the stained-glass makers, and even those of the workmen are recorded. Brewer's " reconstruction " of the interior of this exquisite Chapel is one of the finest of his drawings, Plate 16. The Commons met in St. Stephen's Chapel for 300 years, until its destruction by fire in 1834. The present Houses of Parliament were commenced in 1840.

Westminster Hall, with part of St. Stephen's College and the crypt of the chapel, alone survived that disastrous fire. The Hall was nearly rebuilt by Richard II, but more of the ancient Norman edifice of Rufus was allowed to remain than is usually supposed. What Richard did was simply to heighten the walls, and add new windows and the magnificent roof (the work of the famous carpenter, Hugh Herland) which has stood all these years and was thoroughly repaired in 1923. It is one of the largest halls in the world with a wooden roof unsupported by pillars; its dimensions are: length, 290 feet; width, 68 feet; and height, 92 feet. Unfortunately, much of the original Norman work was obliterated in the restoration of 1825-30, but some interesting portions of the triforium were brought to light in 1923.

Behind Westminster Hall will be seen a number of ancient buildings, forming, with the side of the Hall, a series of irregular open courts. The most important of these was the Exchequer Chamber. It stood on the right-hand side, and only its nearly flat roof is visible. The site occupied by these buildings was cleared in 1882, when the business carried on in them was transferred to the new Law Courts in the Strand, and the long flank of Westminster Hall became open to view.

To the north of Westminster Hall, on its right in the illustration, was and still is New Palace Yard, which in olden times was a vast irregular quadrangle. There was the magnificent and very lofty Richard III Gateway on the west, facing down the yard, and a tall Clock Tower on the north, looking across the yard. In the centre was the Great Conduit. On the side of the New Palace Yard nearest the river (distinguished in the illustration by two ornamental stars on the gables) was the Star Chamber, which gained such discreditable notoriety. An ancient water-gate led from this end of New Palace Yard to the Thames.

The approach to Westminster from the village of Charing is seen in the right-hand top corner of the illustration. It terminated in the narrow road called King Street, which disappeared in 1899, when the present thoroughfare of Parliament Street was widened thereby. King Street came to an abrupt termination with three gates; the first has been already mentioned as giving access to New Palace Yard; the second, or central, one led to the Abbey precincts and the Greater Sanctuary; while the third (on the right coming from Charing) led to the Little Sanctuary. Another gateway is to be seen close by; it led from New Palace Yard into a narrow lane, with gates at each end. This was St. Margaret's Lane, which, passing St. Margaret's Church (on the right of the Abbey), gave access to Old Palace Yard. On the farther side of this yard (on the left in the illustration) was the royal residence.

The large tower was the south gate of the Palace, and the second tower west of the gate was the Jewel Tower, which still exists. Another gateway facing east led into a courtyard, across which was the Parliament Chamber or House of Lords; five windows of the building are shown in the illustration. In 1823 when the Parliament Chamber was demolished the Court of Requests became the House of Lords. It was then found that vaults beneath the Parliament Chamber, called the Guy Fawkes Cellar, had been the kitchen of the Palace. Four of the arches were removed by Sir John Soane to his museum, where they may now be seen. On the left of the House of Lords was the Prince's Chamber and on the right the Painted Chamber, filling opposite sides of the courtyard. The wall paintings which adorned the Painted Chamber dated back to 1237, and were some of the earliest of purely English art. It is related that they were " painted beyond description," but unfortunately the Chamber was destroyed in the fire of 1834 and no portion of these frescoes has been preserved. It may be said to have been the birth-place of the Commons, who went from it to the Chapter House of the Abbey until, after some 300 years, they found another home for 300 years in St. Stephen's Chapel, as already mentioned. In the foreground, between the Painted Chamber and St. Stephen's Chapel, was the Pilgrimage Church of St. Mary-le-Pewe, which was approached from either the one or the other. The name was probably derived from La Puy, in France, where there exists a Pilgrimage Church of Notre-Dame de la Puy.

The buildings of the collegiate establishment of St. Stephen stood to the north (right) of the chapel, and the beautiful old cloisters and double Oratory (seen in the Plate adjoining Westminster Hall to the right of the chapel) were, with the exception of the Jewel Tower, the Crypt of St. Stephen's Chapel, and Westminster Hall, the only portions of the grand old historical Palace which survived. They were the last works executed by Henry VIII before he transferred himself and his court to his new Palace of Whitehall. Oratory and the Hall were slightly damaged in 1940/41.

Westminster Abbey, founded by Edward the Confessor in the 11th century, but rebuilt in the 13th century, is seen without the towers erected in the 18th century. Henry VII's Chapel, which is specially famous for its fantastic fan-vaulting, stands out prominently, and the Chapter House with its flying buttresses may also be noted. The buildings seen to the left of the Abbey are those of the Monastery. They were converted by Queen Elizabeth into St. Peter's College, also known to-day as Westminster School. The old dormitory of the Abbey was used as the great schoolroom, and called "Up School." It suffered severely from enemy action and has now been restored. The old ruins of St. Catherine's Chapel may be seen to-day. The damage received by the Abbey in 1940/41 was not extensive, and the Church was saved by fire-watchers from complete destruction.

The present Houses of Parliament, commenced in 1840, occupy the site of the old Palace of Westminster, including the College of St. Stephen's, but excluding, of course, the Abbey, which is still reckoned part of " Our Palace of Westminster " for coronation purposes. Entering by St. Stephen's porch, we pass Westminster Hall on the left to St. Stephen's Hall, which is built on the Crypt of St. Stephen's Chapel. To reach either the House of Lords or the House of Commons we must then pass on to the Central Hall, from which we turn to the right for the Upper and to the left for the Lower Chamber.

The first house, built after 600 years of temporary homes for the Mother of Parliaments, the House of Commons, was destroyed by enemy action just 100 years later. Yet she flourishes root and branch!

Walk about Zion, and go round about her :
Tell the towers thereof, mark ye well her bulwarks,
  consider her palaces ;
That ye may tell it to the generation following.
For this God is our God for ever and ever.
He will be our guide even unto death.

Index

INDEX (*Continued*)

INDEX (*Continued*)

INDEX (*Continued*)

Plates

Key to main buildings and thoroughfares,
are printed on the reverse of each plate.

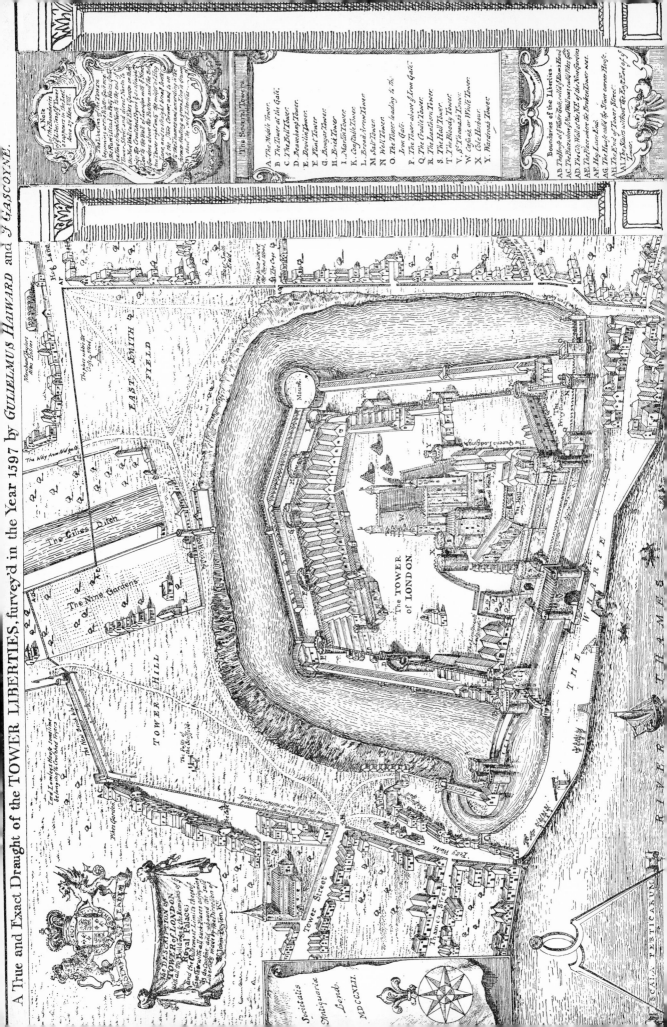

A True and Exact Draught of the TOWER LIBERTIES, surveyd in the Year 1597 by GULIELMUS HAIWARD and J GASCOYNE.

The Severall Towers.

A. The Middle Tower.
B. The Tower at the Gate.
C. The Bell Tower.
D. Beauchamp Tower.
E. Develin Tower.
F. Flint Tower.
G. Bowyer Tower.
H. Brick Tower.
I. Martin Tower.
K. Constable Tower.
L. Broad Arrow Tower.
M. Salt Tower.
N. Well Tower.
O. The Tower leading to the Iron Gate.
P. The Tower above ye Iron Gate.
Q. The Cradle Tower.
R. The Lanthorn Tower.
S. The Hall Tower.
T. The Bloody Tower.
V. S.t Thomas's Tower.
W. Cæsars or White Tower.
X. Cole Harbour.
Y. Wardrobe Tower.

Boundaries of the Liberties.

AB. The House of Water Tank, called St Katherines Head.
AC. The Back way of the Wall that went by that gate.
AD. The Gt. Wall at the NE of the Nine Gardens.
AE. The Place where the Broken Tower next.
AF. Hog Lane End.
AG. The House called the Stone corner House.
AH. The End of Tower Street.
AI. The Stone without the East End of St.

A Note

EAST SMITH FIELD

The place called the Crash stone

The Way from Old gate

The Cities Ditch

The Nine Gardens

TOWER HILL

The Bulwark

The place of the Scaffold

Postern Gate

The TOWER of LONDON

The Queens Stairs

The Iron Gate

Traitors Gate

THE WHARFE

RIVER of THAMES

TOWER Street

Thames Street

Societatis
Antiquariæ
Lond:
MDCCXLII

MERIDIONALIS TRAJECTUS

Plates 1 and 2

THE TOWER OF LONDON (from the south)

All Hallows, Barking	1	30	Byward Tower
Scaffold	2	31	Bell Tower
Tower Hill	3	32	Cold Harbour Gateway
City Wall and Ditch	4	33	Court of The Palace
Postern Gate	5	34	Jewel House
North Bastion	6	35	Queen's Lodgings
The Moat	7	36	Privy Court
Legge's Mount Battery	8	37	Garden or Bloody Tower
Devereaux Tower	9	38	Wakefield Tower
Flint Tower	10	39	Great Hall
Bowyer's Tower	11	40	Lanthorn Tower
Brick Tower	12	41	Salt Tower
Martin Tower	13	42	The Moat
Brass Mount Battery	14	43	St. Thomas's Tower
Menagerie	15	44	King's Gallery
The Moat	16	45	Queen's Gallery
Beauchamp Tower	17	46	Queen's Stairs
Site of Executions	18	47	Traitors' Gate
Church of St. Peter ad Vincula	19	48	The Moat
The Keep	20	49	Cradle Tower
Chapel of St. John	21	50	Privy Garden
Wardrobe Tower	22	51	Well Tower
Inner Wall	23	52	River Thames
Constable Tower	24	53	The Wharf
Lion Tower	25	54	To the Iron Gate
The Wardrobe	26	55	Develin Bridge
Broadarrow Tower	27		
Outer Wall	28		
Middle Tower	29		

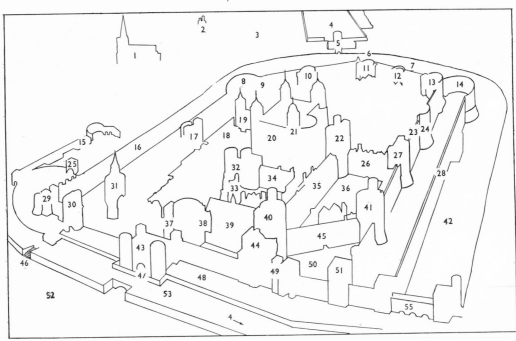

Plate 3

THE CITY OF LONDON AND ENVIRONS (from the east)
Southern Section.

LONDON
IN THE TIME OF HENRY VIII

H.W.BREWER. INV? DEL.   1887.

DEC?

Plate 4

THE CITY OF LONDON AND ENVIRONS (from the east)
Northern Section

Old St. Paul's	1	29	Crosby Hall
Paul's Cross	2	30	Broad Street
City Wall	3	31	St. Helen's
Newgate	4	32	St. Ethelburga's
Ely Place	5	33	St. Botolph's, Bishop's Gate
Greyfriars'	6	34	St. Mary of Bethlehem
St. Bartholomew the Great	7	35	St. Mary of Spital
The Charterhouse	8	36	St. Olave's, Hart Street
St. John's, Clerkenwell	9	37	Fore Church
St. James's Priory, Clerkenwell	10	38	Fenchurch Street
Hampstead	11	39	St. Katherine Cree
Highgate	12	40	Holy Trinity
Bow Church	13	41	St. Botolph's, Aldgate
Cheapside	14	42	Hound's Ditch
St. Peter	15	43	Scaffold
Aldersgate	16	44	Postern Gate
The Guildhall	17	45	East Minster
Austin Friars'	18	46	City Wall and Ditch
St. Giles, Cripplegate	19	47	St. Clare of the Minories
Barbican	20		
Moorgate	21		
Moorfields	22		
Conduit	23		
St. Christopher-le-Stocks	24		
The Leadenhall	25		
St. Andrew's, Undershaft	26		
SS. Mary and Ursula	27		
Bishopsgate Street	28		

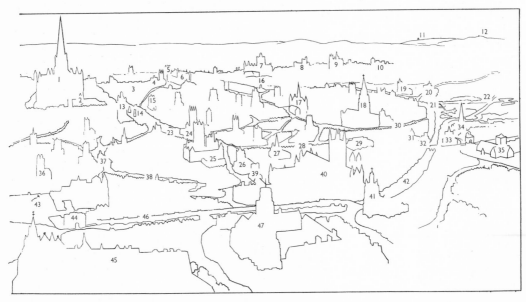

44

Plate 5

OLD LONDON BRIDGE (from the south)

St. Magnus-the-Martyr	1	20	Bridge House
The Tower of London	2	21	Heads and Limbs
Fishmongers' Hall	3	22	Roger Lock
Waterworks	4	23	Traitors' Gate
King's Lock	5	24	Southwark Flourmills
London Square	6	25	The Pillory
Chapel of St. Thomas à Becket	7	26	The Refectory
Nonesuch House	8	27	Church of St. Mary Overy
Queen's Lock	9	28	The Lady Chapel
St. Mary's Lock	10	29	The Bishop's Chapel
Chapel Lock	11	30	Winchester House
Sterling	12	31	St. Saviour's Dock
Long Entry Lock	13	32	Priory Gate
Great Lock	14	33	West Entrance
Nonesuch Lock	15	34	St. Mary Magdalene's Church
Drawbridge	16		
River Thames	17		
Sterling	18		
Draw Lock	19		

SAINT PAVL'S CATHEDRAL

Before the destruction of the Spire.
Restored from Ancient Authorities
By H. W. Brewer. 1891

Plate 6

OLD ST. PAUL'S (from the north-east)

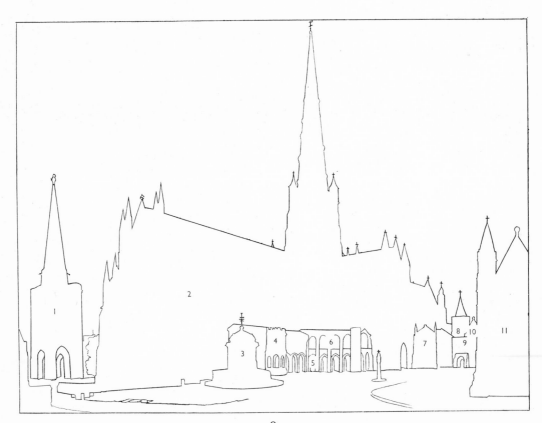

H W Brewer 1884

Plate 7

OLD ST. PAUL'S: THE NAVE AND EAST END

Plate 8

OLD ST. PAUL'S: THE EAST END

Plate 9

OLD ST. PAUL'S: THE NORTH AISLE OF THE EAST END

* *The Tablet and Mutilated Effigies from these Monuments are in the Crypt of the present Cathedral.*

Plate 10

CHEAPSIDE (from the east)

Plate 11

LUDGATE (from the west)

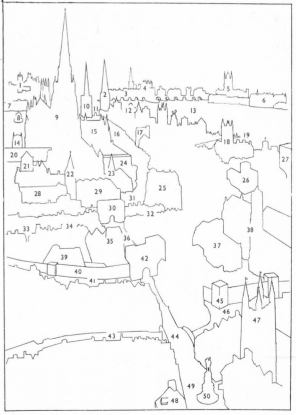

H.W. Brewer 1894

Plate 12

NEWGATE (from the west)

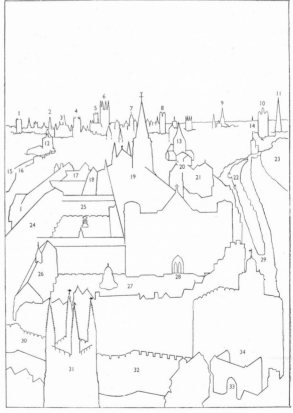

Plate 13

ALDGATE (from the west)

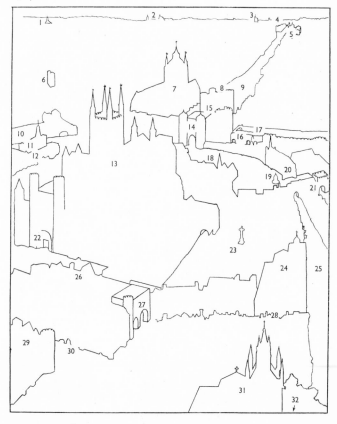

Plate 14

ELY PLACE (from the west)

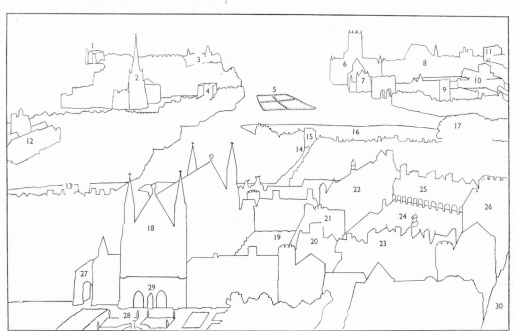

Plate 15

WESTMINSTER (from the east)

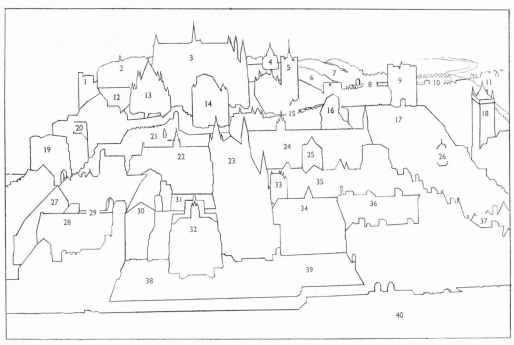

H.W.Brewer 1892.

Plate 16

WESTMINSTER: ST. STEPHEN'S CHAPEL

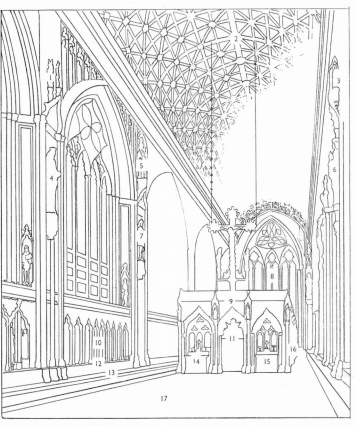